Tom's Friend

Written and Illustrated
by Pat Reynolds

"Mum! Where are you? Look what I've found!"
Tom came running up to the back door,
excited and out of breath.

"He was by the long grass near the back fence.
Probably lives in the bushes along the creek.
He likes me, Mum. Look, you can tell —
he's smiling. And he didn't run away.
I was very gentle with him.
He didn't mind when I picked him up.
He likes me and I want to keep him . . ."

"What have you got there?" asked his mum.

Tom held out the bucket she used
to water her plants.
Curled up in the bottom was a big lizard.
It didn't fit in the bucket very well,
and it looked up at them awkwardly
with one bright eye.

"Look at his nose holes," said Tom.
He pointed into the bucket,
but his hand shot back again
when the lizard threw open its mouth
and revealed a very blue tongue.

"Why did he do that?" Tom was shocked
that his new friend had been unfriendly.

"You frightened him, so he tried to scare you off.
That's how he protects himself from dogs
and cats and big birds."

"Well it's a good trick!" said Tom.
"He must be a bluetongue lizard.
I think I'll call him Bluey. He can be my new pet.
I'm going to make him a home right now.
This bucket is too small." And he rushed off.

"Wait a minute . . ." called Mum.

But Tom didn't hear her, and she went inside
with a half-smile, half-frown on her face.

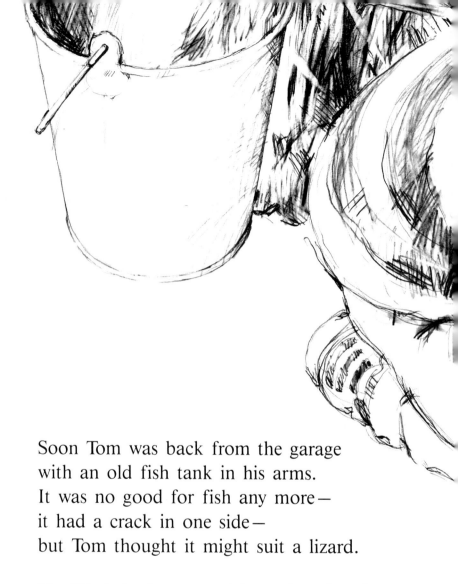

Soon Tom was back from the garage
with an old fish tank in his arms.
It was no good for fish any more —
it had a crack in one side —
but Tom thought it might suit a lizard.

He filled the bottom with sand and rocks.
Then he put a dish in one corner, for water,
and planted some tufts of grass in the other.

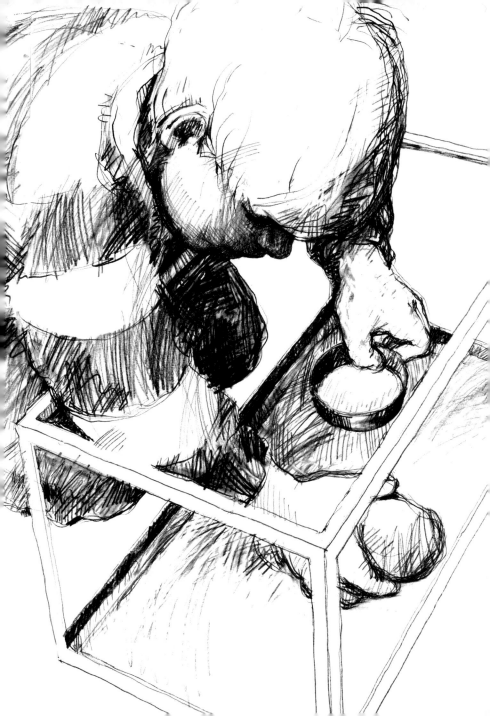

"It's ready, Mum," he called.

He put on one of her gardening gloves,
just to be safe, and gently carried the lizard
from the bucket to the glass tank.
"There you go, Bluey," he murmured.

Mum came out to have a look.
Tom had certainly tried hard
to make a good home for the lizard.

"See," he said, very pleased with himself.
"He can move around now.
He has water to drink,
and somewhere to hide under that grass.
What do lizards eat, Mum?
Insects and things like that?"

"Yes, I think so. And fruit."

"Do you think he would eat minced steak?"

"Probably."

But there was something wrong.
Mum didn't look happy.

"Did I forget something?" Tom asked.

"Well, yes and no," said Mum
with that same half-smile, half-frown.

Tom protested. "He has everything he needs.
What have I forgotten?"

"Come with me, Tom."

She held his hand and they walked down
to the bottom of the backyard.
"Show me where you found the lizard."

"Here. He was sitting in the sun
next to this long grass."

"Tom," said Mum, "I want you to imagine
that you're a lizard, and tell me
what you're going to do today."

Tom's eyes lit up. "O.K.," he said.
"Well, first I'm going to lie
in the sun here for a while.
Then I'll creep down there,
through the long grass,
to the creek for a drink. Then . . .
I think I'll catch some fat ants for lunch,
over there where they live in that mound.
And now I'll stretch out on that big flat rock
over there, by the water, and have
my after-lunch nap."

"I might go for a walk up the creek
after that, to see what's there,
since you never let me go that far,
and then . . ."

"Let's go back to the house now," said Mum.
And they walked back, with Tom pulling her
up the hill because she always pretended
to be out of breath.

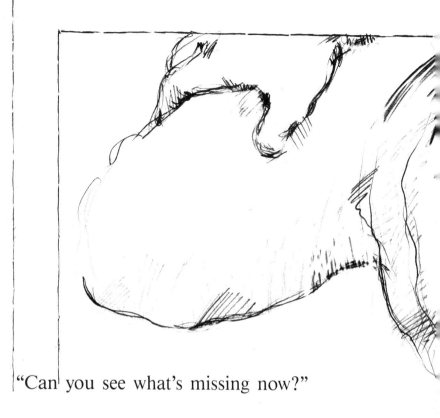

"Can you see what's missing now?"

Tom looked at the lizard in the tank
and his face grew sad.
He knew what she meant.

"I think I'd better let him go, Mum," he said.

Mum squeezed his hand.
"I think Bluey really likes you for that.
Look, he's smiling!"